CONTENTS

NAMES *of* GOD

ADONAI

Meaning
The Lord; My Great Lord

Application
God is the Master and majestic Lord. God is our total authority.

Bible Reference
Psalm 8; Isaiah 40:3–5; Ezekiel 16:8; Habakkuk 3:19

Comments
Pronounced: ah-doe-NI
Adonai (plural) is derived from the singular *Adon* (Lord). This term was pronounced in substitution of *YHWH* (considered too sacred to be uttered).

EL

Meaning
The Strong One

Application
He is more powerful than any false god. God will overcome all obstacles. We can depend on God.

Bible Reference
Exodus 15:2; Numbers 23:22; Deuteronomy 7:9 (Mark 15:34)

Comments
Pronounced: el
Occurs more than 200 times in the Old Testament (including compounds). Generic Semitic name for God, used by other cultures to refer to their gods. *El* is used in compound proper names such as Isra-*el* (wrestles with God), Beth-*el* (House of God), and *El*-isha (God is salvation).

El Elohe Yisrael

Meaning
God, the God of Israel

Application
The God of Israel is distinct and separate from all false gods of the world.

Bible Reference
Genesis 33:20; Exodus 5:1; Psalm 68:8; 106:48

Comments
Pronounced: el el-o-HAY yis-raw-ALE
The name of the altar that Jacob (Israel) erected after his encounter with God and God's blessing upon him. (Genesis 32:24–30; 33:19–20)

EL ELYON

Meaning
The God Most High

Application
He is the Sovereign God in whom we can put our trust. El Elyon has supremacy over all false gods.

Bible Reference
Genesis 14:17–22; Psalm 78:35; Daniel 4:34 (Acts 16:17)

Comments
Pronounced: el EL-yuhn
Melchizedek, the king of Salem (Jeru "Salem") and the priest of God Most High, referred to God as "El Elyon" three times when he blessed Abram.

Elohim

Meaning
The All-Powerful One; Creator

Application
God is the all-powerful creator of the universe. God knows all, creates all, and is everywhere at all times. The plural of "El."

Bible Reference
Genesis 1:1–3; Deuteronomy 10:17; Psalm 68 (Mark 13:19)

Comments
Pronounced: el-o-HEEM
Plural form of *El.* This name is usually associated with God in relation to his creation. Some people use the plural word "Elohim" as proof for the Trinity (Genesis 1:26). *Elohim* is also used to refer to false gods and even human judges (Psalm 82:6–7; John 10:34).

EL OLAM

Meaning
The Eternal God; The Everlasting God

Application
He is the beginning and the end, the one who works his purposes throughout the ages. He gives strength to the weary.

Bible Reference
Genesis 21:33; Psalm 90:1–2; Isaiah 40:28 (Romans 1:20)

Comments
Pronounced: el o-LAHM
Jesus Christ possesses eternal attributes. He is the same yesterday and today and forever (Hebrews 13:8). He obtained eternal redemption for us (Hebrews 9:12).

El Roi

Meaning
The God Who Sees Me

Application
There are no circumstances in our lives that escape his fatherly awareness and care. God knows us and our troubles.

Bible Reference
Genesis 16:11–14; Psalm 139:7–12

Comments
Pronounced: el ROY
Hagar called the Lord by this name beside a fountain of water in the wilderness. God knows all of our thoughts and feelings. Jesus knew the thoughts of those around him, demonstrating that he is *El Roi* (Matthew 22:18; 26:21, 34; Luke 5:21–24).

EL SHADDAI

Meaning
The All Sufficient One; The God of the Mountains; God Almighty

Application
God is the all-sufficient source of all of our blessings. God is all-powerful. Our problems are not too big for God to handle.

Bible Reference
Genesis 17:1–3; 35:11; 48:3; 49:25; Psalm 90:2

Comments
Pronounced: el-shaw-DIE
Some scholars suggest that *Shaddai* refers to God's power evident in his judgment. Others suggest that *El Shaddai* means "God of the Mountains." God refers to himself as "El Shaddai" when he confirms his covenant with Abraham.

IMMANUEL

Meaning
God With Us; "I AM"

Application
Jesus is God in our midst. In him all the
fullness of Deity dwells in bodily form.

Bible Reference
Isaiah 7:14; 8.8–10 (Matthew 1:23)

Comments
Pronounced: ih-MAN-u-el
This name indicates that Jesus is more than
man. He is also God. Isaiah said that the
child born to the virgin would be called
"Immanuel" (Isaiah 7:14; 9:6). He is the
radiance of God's glory and the exact
representation of his nature (Hebrews 1:3).

JEHOVAH

Meaning
"I AM"; The One Who Is; The Self-Existent One

Application
God never changes. His promises never fail. When we are faithless, he is faithful. We need to obey him.

Bible Reference
Exodus 3:14; 6:2–4; 34:5–7; Psalm 102

Comments
Pronounced: juh-HO-vah
A sixteenth-century German translator wrote the name YHVH (YHWH) using the vowels of *Adonai*, because the ancient Jewish texts from which he was translating had the vowels of *Adonai* under the consonants of YHVH. By doing this, he incorrectly came up with the name Jehovah (*YaHoVaH*).

JEHOVAH-JIREH

Meaning
The Lord Will Provide

Application
Just as God provided a ram as a substitute for Isaac, he provided his son Jesus as the ultimate sacrifice. God will meet all our needs.

Bible Reference
Genesis 22:13–14; Psalm 23; (Mark 10:45; Romans 8:2)

Comments
Pronounced: juh-HO-vah JI-rah
Also known as YHWH-Jireh. Abraham called the place "the Lord will provide" where God provided a ram to be sacrificed instead of his son Isaac. Jesus said that he was the bread of life and anyone who comes to him will be provided for (John 6:35).

JEHOVAH-MEKADDISHKEM

Meaning
The Lord Who Sanctifies

Application
God sets us apart as a chosen people, a royal priesthood, holy unto God, a people of his own. He cleanses our sin and helps us mature.

Bible Reference
Exodus 31:12–13 (1 Peter 1:15–16; Hebrews 13:12; 1 Thessalonians 5:23–24)

Comments
Pronounced: juh-HO-vah mek-KAH-dish-KIM

Also known as YHWH-Mekaddishkem. We have been set apart, made holy, and redeemed by the blood of Jesus Christ, our *Jehovah-Mekaddishkem*. Therefore, we are to continue to live our lives holy and pleasing to God (1 Peter 1:13–25).

JEHOVAH-NISSI

Meaning
The Lord Is My Banner

Application
God gives us victory against the flesh, the world and the devil. Our battles are his battles of light against darkness and good against evil.

Bible Reference
Exodus 17:15-16; Deuteronomy 20:3-4; Isaiah 11:10–12 (Ephesians 6:10–18)

Comments
Pronounced: juh-HO-vah NEE-see
Also known as YHWH-Nissi. Name of the altar built by Moses after defeating the Amalekites at Rephidim. Isaiah prophesies that the "Root of Jesse" (Jesus) will stand as a banner for the peoples (Isaiah 11:10).

17

JEHOVAH-RAPHA

Meaning
The Lord Who Heals

Application
God has provided the final cure for spiritual, physical, and emotional sickness in Jesus Christ. God can heal us.

Bible Reference
Exodus 15:25–27; Psalm 103:3; 147:3
(1 Peter 2:24)

Comments
Pronounced: juh-HO-vah RAH-fah
Also known as YHWH-Rapha. Jesus demonstrated that He was *Jehovah-Rapha* in his healing of the sick, blind, lame, and casting out demons. Jesus also heals his people from sin and unrighteousness (Luke 5:31–32).

JEHOVAH-ROHI

Meaning
The Lord Is My Shepherd

Application
The Lord protects, provides, directs, leads, and cares for his people. God tenderly takes care of us as a strong and patient shepherd.

Bible Reference
Psalm 23:1–3; Isaiah 53:6 (John 10:14–18; Hebrews 13:20; Revelation 7:17)

Comments
Pronounced: juh-HO-vah RO-hee
Also known as YHWH-Ra'ah (RAH-ah). Jesus is the good shepherd who lays down his life for all people.

JEHOVAH-SABAOTH

Meaning
The Lord of Hosts; The Lord of Armies

Application
The Lord of the hosts of heaven will always fulfill his purposes, even when the hosts of his earthly people fail.

Bible Reference
1 Samuel 1:3; 17:45; Psalm 46:7; Malachi 1:10–14 (Romans 9:29)

Comments
Pronounced: juh-HO-vah sah-bah-OATH
Also known as YHWH-Sabaoth. Many English versions of the Bible translate *Sabaoth* as "Almighty." "Jehovah-Sabaoth" is often translated as "*The Lord Almighty.*" *Sabaoth* is also translated as "*Heavenly Hosts*" or "*Armies.*"

JEHOVAH-SHALOM

Meaning
The Lord Is Peace

Application
God defeats our enemies to bring us peace.
Jesus is our Prince of Peace. God brings inner
peace and harmony.

Bible Reference
Numbers 6:22–27; Judges 6:22–24;
Isaiah 9:6 (Hebrews 13:20)

Comments
Pronounced: juh-HO-vah shah-LOME
Also known as YHWH-Shalom. Name
of the altar built by Gideon at Ophrah to
memorialize God's message "Peace be unto
thee." Isaiah tells us that the Messiah will
also be known as the "Prince of Peace," our
Jehovah-Shalom (Isaiah 9:6).

JEHOVAH-SHAMMAH

Meaning
The Lord Is There; The Lord My Companion

Application
God's presence is not limited or contained in the tabernacle or temple, but is accessible to all who love and obey him.

Bible Reference
Ezekiel 48:35; Psalm 46 (Matthew 28:20; Revelation 21)

Comments
Pronounced: juh-HO-vah SHAHM-mah
Also known as YHWH-Shammah. God revealed to Ezekiel that the name of the New Jerusalem shall be "The LORD is there." Through Jesus Christ, the Spirit of God dwells in us (1 Corinthians 3:16).

JEHOVAH-TSIDKENU

Meaning
The Lord Our Righteousness

Application
Jesus is the King who would come from David's line, and is the one who imparts his righteousness to us.

Bible Reference
Jeremiah 23:5–6; 33:16; Ezekiel 36:26–27 (2 Corinthians 5:21)

Comments
Pronounced: juh-HO-vah tsid-KAY-noo
Also known as YHWH-Tsidkenu. All people sin and fall short of God's glory, but God freely makes us righteous through faith in Jesus Christ (Romans 3:22–23). God promised to send a King who will reign wisely and do what is just and right. The people will live in safety (Jeremiah 23:5–6).

YAH, OR JAH

Meaning
"I AM"; The One Who Is; The Self-Existent One

Application
God never changes. His promises never fail. When we are faithless, he is faithful. God promises his continuing presence.

Bible Reference
Exodus 3:14; 15:2; Psalm 46:1; 68:4; Isaiah 26:4

Comments
Pronounced: Yah

Shorter form of *Yahweh*. It is often used when combined with other names or phrases. *Hallelujah* means "Praise Yah (the Lord)," *Elijah* means "God is Yah (the Lord)," and *Joshua* means "Yah (the Lord) is my salvation."

YHWH

Meaning
"I AM"; The One Who Is; The Self-Existent One

Application
God never changes. His promises never fail. When we are faithless, he is faithful.

Bible Reference
Exodus 3.14; Malachi 3:6

Comments
Pronounced: YAH-way

God's personal name given to Moses. Also called the tetragrammaton ("four letters"). Occurs about 6,800 times. Translated "LORD" in English versions of the Bible, because it became common practice for Jews to say "Lord" (Adonai) instead of saying the name *YHWH*.

NAMES *of* JESUS

ALMIGHTY

Meaning
Jesus is all-powerful.

Application
Christ is the all-powerful Lord. Nothing is
beyond his reach or impossible for him.

Bible Reference
Revelation 1:8

Related Titles
Mighty God (Isaiah 9:6)
Mighty in Battle (Psalm 24:8)
Potentate (Ruler) (1 Timothy 6:15)
Power of God (1 Corinthians 1:24)

AUTHOR AND FINISHER

Meaning
Jesus is our start and finish.

Application
Jesus was at the beginning of creation and will be there to the end. He is both the author of all that is and the one who sees his creation through to the end.

Bible Reference
Hebrews 12:2

Related Titles
Alpha and Omega, Beginning and End, First and Last (Revelation 1:8; 21:6; 22:13)

BELOVED

Meaning
Jesus is at the center of God's love.

Application
Christ is the Beloved Son of the Father, and as such, the desire of all people who love God. All who love God will be drawn to Jesus.

Bible Reference
Ephesians 1:6

Related Titles
Desire of all nations (Haggai 2:7)
Associate of God (Zechariah 13:7)

BRANCH

Meaning
Jesus is the shoot from David's line.

Application
Jesus is the offshoot of the line of David and paradoxically also the root. He is the vine on which we depend for life and nourishment.

Bible Reference
Isaiah 11:1; Jeremiah 23:5; Zechariah 3:8; 6:12

Related Titles
Nazarene (Netzer = Branch in Hebrew; Matthew 2:23; Isaiah 11:1)
Root of David, Shoot, Vine (Revelation 5:5; Isaiah 11:10; 53:2; John 15:1)

BREAD OF LIFE

Meaning
Jesus is our sustenance.

Application
Jesus was born in Bethlehem, which means "the house of bread." He is our spiritual nourishment and the sustenance of the world. All things are kept alive by him.

Bible Reference
John 6:32–35

Related Titles
Living Bread (John 6:5)
Living Water (John 7:37–38)

BRIDEGROOM

Meaning
Jesus leads and cares for us.

Application
Jesus is the bridegroom and his church is the bride. He is the head of the church and cares for her.

Bible Reference
Matthew 9:15; John 3:29; Revelation 21:9

Related Titles
Head of the Church (Ephesians 5:23)
Head of the Body (Ephesians 4:15–16)

BRIGHT MORNING STAR

Meaning
Jesus lights our way.

Application
Jesus is the brightest star in the heavens and the light of the world. We shall not lose our way in his light.

Bible Reference
Revelation 22:16

Related Titles
Day Star (2 Peter 1:19)
Star (Numbers 24:17)
Sunrise (Luke 1:78)
Sun of Righteousness (Malachi 4:2)

CARPENTER

Meaning
Jesus is one of us.

Application
Jesus, the creator of wood, became a worker of wood, and died on a cross of wood for us (Galatians 3:13).

Bible Reference
Mark 6:3

Related Titles
Carpenter's Son (Matthew 13:55)

CHOSEN ONE

Meaning
Jesus is God's Chosen One.

Application
Jesus is God's chosen one, chosen for glory and great sacrifice. We, in him, are God's chosen people.

Bible Reference
Luke 23:35

Related Titles
Elect One (Isaiah 42:1)

CHIEF CORNERSTONE

Meaning
Jesus is our rock of safety.

Application
Jesus is the cornerstone which the religious leaders rejected, but which God chose from eternity to build his house, a temple of living stone! We can rely on him as our solid foundation.

Bible Reference
Isaiah 28:16; Psalm 118:22; Ephesians 2:20; 1 Peter 2:6

Related Titles
Foundation (1 Corinthians 3:11)
Living Stone (1 Peter 2:4)
Precious Stone (Isaiah 28:16)
Rock (1 Corinthians 10:4)
Rock of Offense (1 Peter 2:8)
Stone (Psalm 118:22)

DOOR

Meaning
Jesus is our gateway.

Application
Jesus is our opening to God. He is the only way to heaven.

Bible Reference
John 10:9

Related Titles
Door of the Sheepfold (John 10:7)

EMMANUEL/ IMMANUEL

Meaning
Jesus is God with us.

Application
Jesus was born on earth as a real human being. He entered space and time to become one of us so we might be with God forever.

Bible Reference
Isaiah 7:14—8:8; Matthew 1:23

Related Titles
Only Begotten God (John 1:18)

ETERNAL FATHER

Meaning
Jesus is forever.

Application
Christ had no beginning and has no end. He is the source of time, space, and all creation.

Bible Reference
Isaiah 9:6; 1 John 1:1–3

Related Titles
Head of the Creation of God
(Revelation 3:14)

FAITHFUL AND TRUE WITNESS

Meaning
Jesus is faithful.

Application
Christ is Truth in the flesh. His witness is always faithful. We can trust his word.

Bible Reference
Revelation 1:5; 3:14

Related Titles
Amen (Revelation 3:14)
Faithful and True (Revelation 19:11)
Truth (John 14:6)

FIRSTBORN

Meaning
Jesus is our elder brother.

Application
Christ is the firstborn of the dead, the first-fruits of a new humanity, resurrected in new form. As our eldest brother, he is heir of all things (Hebrews 2:11). (The importance of the firstborn is also connected to Passover. At the Exodus, the firstborn child of the Hebrews was "passed over." He was saved from death by the sacrifice of a lamb.)

Bible Reference
Hebrews 12:23; Revelation 5

Related Titles
First-fruits (1 Corinthians 15:20)
Firstborn from the Dead (Colossians 1:18)

GOD

Meaning
Jesus is God.

Application
Christ is in his very nature God and all the fullness of that essence is in him. He is worthy of our worship.

Bible Reference
John 1:1, 14–18; Romans 9:5; Titus 2:13; Hebrews 1:8

Related Titles
Fullness of God (Colossians 2:9)

HEAD OF THE CHURCH

Meaning
Jesus leads the church.

Application
Jesus is the leader and Lord of the church. True believers will follow him as he cares for them and directs their way.

Bible Reference
Ephesians 5:23

Related Titles
Head of the Body (Ephesians 4:15–16)

HIGH PRIEST, APOSTLE

Meaning
Jesus is our prophet and priest.

Application
An apostle is someone who has directly communicated with God and is authorized to speak for him. A high priest is God's appointed person to represent the people to himself. Jesus is both God's spokesman and our representative to God.

Bible Reference
Hebrews 3:1–2

Related Titles
Bishop of Souls (1 Peter 2:25)
Minister of the Sanctuary (Hebrews 8:1–2)
The Prophet (Deuteronomy 18:15–18;
    John 6:14)

HOLY ONE

Meaning
Jesus is perfect.

Application
Christ is without sin and evil. Because of this, he became the only perfect man to walk upon the earth. Therefore, he is the only one who could die to save us.

Bible Reference
Mark 1:24; Acts 2:27; 3:14; Psalm 16:10

Related Titles
Holy Child (Servant) (Acts 4:30)
Lord Our Righteousness (Jeremiah 23:5–6)
Righteous One (1 John 2:1)
Sanctification (1 Corinthians 1:30)

HOPE

Meaning
Jesus is our confidence.

Application
Jesus is our only source of hope in the world.
His conquest of death gives us confidence
now and for the future.

Bible Reference
1 Timothy 1:1

Related Titles
Hope of Glory (Colossians 1:27)
Hope of Israel (Jeremiah 17:13)

IMAGE OF THE INVISIBLE GOD

Meaning
Jesus is the perfect picture of God.

Application
Because Christ and the Father are one in nature, Jesus perfectly reflects God. When we look at him, we see what God looks like as a man.

Bible Reference
2 Corinthians 4:4; Colossians 1:15

Related Titles
Exact Representation of his Nature (Hebrews 1:3)

JESUS

Meaning
Jesus saves.

Application
Jesus is the Greek form of the Hebrew *Yeshua* (Joshua). The name means "Yahweh (Jehovah) is salvation."

Bible Reference
Matthew 1:21

Related Titles
Yeshua (Joshua)

JUDGE, RULER

Meaning
Jesus is our judge as well as our advocate and lawyer.

Application
Jesus, the very one who is our advocate before the bar of God's justice, has been made the Judge of all (Romans 8:33–34).

Bible Reference
John 5:22–23; Micah 4:3; Matthew 26:67; Acts 10:42

Related Titles
See *Wonderful Counselor*

KING OF KINGS

Meaning
Jesus is king over all.

Application
Christ is the king over all kings and rulers.
As subjects in his kingdom, we owe him our
complete allegiance.

Bible Reference
Revelation 17:14

Related Titles
King (Matthew 21:5)
King of Israel (John 1:49)
King of the Jews (Matthew 2:2)
Lord of Lords (Revelation 19:16)
Master (Luke 8:24)
Prince (Daniel 9:25)
Ruler Sovereign (1 Timothy 6:15)

LAMB OF GOD

Meaning
Jesus is our sacrifice.

Application
Jesus is the fulfillment of the whole sacrificial system, especially as our Passover Lamb (Hebrews 7:26–29). As the Lamb of God, Jesus' sacrifice pays for our sins past, present, and future.

Bible Reference
John 1:29, 36; 1 Peter 1:19;
Revelation 5:6–12; 7:17

Related Titles
Offering (Hebrews 10:10)
Passover (1 Corinthians 5:7)
Propitiation (1 John 2:2)
Sacrifice (Ephesians 5:2)

Last Adam

Meaning
Jesus is the Father of a new human nature.

Application
The first Adam brought sin and death. Jesus is the Last Adam, bringing life. From him flows eternal life.

Bible Reference
1 Corinthians 15:45

Related Titles
Man, Second Man, Son of Man
 (Daniel 7:13–14; Mark 9:31; John 19:5;
 1 Timothy 2:5)

LIGHT OF THE WORLD

Meaning
Jesus is the light.

Application
Jesus' radiance reveals God. Knowing Jesus is to know and see what God is like. Those who follow him will not walk in darkness (John 8:12).

Bible Reference
John 8:12

Related Titles
Light (John 1:4–5)
Radiance of God's Glory (Hebrews 1:3)

LION OF THE TRIBE OF JUDAH

Meaning
Jesus is David's son.

Application
Jesus fulfills the Old Testament prophecies, being from the tribe of Judah and the lineage of David.

Bible Reference
Genesis 49:9–10; Revelation 5:5

Related Titles
Son of David (Matthew 12:23)

LIVING WATER SPIRIT

Meaning
Jesus is our spiritual drink.

Application
Christ is the fountainhead of the life
that wells up inside every believer like an
unending spring.

Bible Reference
John 4:10; 7:38

Related Titles
Fountain, Life-Giving Spirit (Jeremiah 2:13;
   Zechariah 13:1; 1 Corinthians 15:45)

LORD OF LORDS

Meaning
Jesus is Lord.

Application
Jesus is Lord over all! He has this title by right as the Son of God and Creator of the cosmos. It is also a title he has earned by his humble work of becoming human in order to redeem us through his death.

Bible Reference
Revelation 19:16; 1 Timothy 6:15

Related Titles
Lord (Philippians 2:11)

MAN OF SORROWS

Meaning
Jesus bore our sorrows.

Application
Jesus did not come to enjoy a life of happy kingship over the world. He came to carry the world's sins and sorrows, that we might have eternal joy with him and God the Father.

Bible Reference
Isaiah 53:3

Related Titles
Servant, Slave (Isaiah 42:1–2; 49:7; 52:13–53:12; Matthew 12:18–20)

MASTER

Meaning
Jesus is our teacher.

Application
Master means "teacher" or "rabbi." Jesus is the final source of truth concerning God. He is the only teacher who can show us the way to go.

Bible Reference
Matthew 8:19

Related Titles
Rabbi, Rabboni, Teacher, Truth (John 14:6–7; 20:16)

MESSENGER OF THE COVENANT

Meaning
Jesus is God's final messenger.

Application
Messenger and *angel* are the same word in both the Old and New Testaments. Christ is God's ultimate messenger of the new covenant of God's grace and head of God's angelic armies.

Bible Reference
Malachi 3:1

Related Titles
Angel of the Lord (Exodus 3:2;
    Judges 13:15–18)
Captain of the Lord's Host (Joshua 5:14)

MESSIAH

Meaning
Jesus is Messiah.

Application
Messiah is the Hebrew word, translated into Greek, as *Christ*. Both words mean "anointed one" (one especially appointed by God for his plan and purpose).

Bible Reference
Daniel 9:25; John 1:41; 4:25

Related Titles
Christ (Matthew 1:16)
Anointed One (Psalm 2:1–2)

PRINCE OF PEACE

Meaning
Jesus is our peace.

Application
Christ is our peace. He has ended the conflict between God and man by his death on the cross. He has also given us internal peace by the love that is planted in our hearts by his Spirit.

Bible Reference
Isaiah 9:6

Related Titles
Peace (Ephesians 2:14)
King of Salem (Hebrews 7:1–2)

PROPHET

Meaning
Jesus is the prophet foretold.

Application
Long before Jesus was born, Moses and others prophesied that a prophet like him would come speaking God's words. Jesus is that Prophet, the ultimate and final spokesman for God.

Bible Reference
John 6:14; 7:40; Deuteronomy 18:15–22; Luke 7:16; Matthew 21:11

Related Titles
See *High Priest*

REDEEMER

Meaning
Jesus is our redemption.

Application
Christ's death is the payment that redeems us from the debt we owe to God's law, ransoming our lives and guaranteeing us a place in his family.

Bible Reference
Job 19:25

Related Titles
Kinsman (Ruth 2:14)
Ransom (Matthew 20:28; 1 Timothy 2:6)
Redemption (1 Corinthians 1:30)
Guarantee (Hebrews 7:22)

RESURRECTION AND THE LIFE

Meaning
Jesus is life.

Application
Christ is life itself. Death could not hold him, nor can it hold any who are in him.

Bible Reference
John 11:25

Related Titles
Living One (Revelation 1:18)

SAVIOR

Meaning
Jesus is our salvation.

Application
Christ is the Savior of the world, come to deliver us from the power of death. He is the one who seeks and saves the lost.

Bible Reference
Luke 1:47—2:11; John 4:42;
1 John 4:14

Related Titles
Captain of Salvation (Hebrews 2:10)
Deliverer (Romans 11:26)
Horn of Salvation (Luke 1:69)
Salvation (Luke 2:30)

SHEPHERD

Meaning
Jesus is the good shepherd.

Application
Jesus came to care for and to lead lost sheep, lost men and women. His sheep know his voice and no one can take them from his hands.

Bible Reference
1 Peter 2:25

Related Titles
Door of the Sheepfold (John 10:7)
Good Shepherd (John 10:14)

SHILOH

Meaning
Jesus is our promised peace.

Application
Shiloh may be translated as "to whom the scepter belongs," or as a name derived from the Hebrew word for peace. Jesus fulfills the prophecy by being the King to whom the scepter belongs and our Prince of Peace.

Bible Reference
Genesis 49:10

Related Titles
See *Messiah* and *Prince of Peace*

SON OF GOD

Meaning
Jesus is the Son of God by nature.

Application
Christ is the only "natural" Son of God, which means he partakes in the Divine nature fully. We become God's children by adoption and inherit all creation in, and with, Christ.

Bible Reference
Luke 1:35; Hebrews 4:14

Related Titles
Only Begotten (John 1:14, 18)
Son of the Most High (Luke 1:32)
Heir (Hebrews 1:2)

TRUE VINE

Meaning
Jesus is our evergreen source of life.

Application
Jesus is our connection to the source of life. As God he has life in himself. Having become a man he extends that life to all who believe.

Bible Reference
John 15:1

Related Titles
See *Branch*

THE WAY, THE TRUTH, AND THE LIFE

Meaning
Jesus is our path to God.

Application
Jesus is the way to God. He is the path to truth and life. No mere human teacher, he is the map, the road, the destination, and the one who has gone ahead of us.

Bible Reference
John 14:6; Acts 9:2

Related Titles
Forerunner (Hebrews 6:20)
Jacob's Ladder (Genesis 28:12; John 1:51)

WISDOM OF GOD

Meaning
Jesus is our wisdom from God.

Application
Though the reference in Proverbs is not a strict prophetic word about Christ, the concept of wisdom as a person and associate of God is fulfilled in Jesus. To know Jesus is to be connected to the wisdom of the ages.

Bible Reference
1 Corinthians 1:24, 30

Related Titles
Compare personified wisdom
   (Proverbs 8:22–31; Luke 11:49)

WONDERFUL COUNSELOR

Meaning
Jesus is our defense attorney.

Application
Christ is our Wonderful Counselor before
God. He comforts, consoles, and counsels
us as our mediator and intercessor. As our
advocate before God, he defends us like a
lawyer before the bar of God's justice, offering
himself as a payment for our crimes.

Bible Reference
Isaiah 9:6

Related Titles
Advocate (1 John 2:1)
Comforter (Paraclete) (John 14:16)
Consolation of Israel (Luke 2:25)
Daysman (Mediator, Intercessor) (Job 9:33;
    1 Timothy 2:5)

WORD

Meaning
Jesus is God's Word.

Application
Jesus is the speech uttered by God the Father, impelled by the breath of God's Spirit. He is not merely information, but the effective, powerful Word that calls creation out of nothing and life out of death.

Bible Reference
John 1:1, 14

Related Titles
Word of God, Word of Life (1 John 1:1)

YAHWEH (JEHOVAH*)

Meaning
Jesus has God's name.

Application
The holy name *Yahweh* means "He who is."
It expresses the idea that only God has self-existent being. The name was so holy that
the Jews would not utter it out loud. Christ
possesses this name.

Bible Reference
Isaiah 40:3–5; Matthew 3:3; 28:19;
Philippians 2:6–11; Exodus 3:14

Related Titles
I AM, Who Was, Who Is, and Who Is to
Come (Mark 6:50; Luke 21:8; John 8:24, 28,
58; Revelation 4:8)

*Using the vowels of *Adonai* (Lord) and the
consonants of *YHVH* (God), a sixteenth-century
German translator incorrectly translated *YHVH* as
YaHoVah, resulting in the name *Jehovah*. Yahweh is
the more accepted spelling for God's name.

NAMES *of the* HOLY SPIRIT

BREATH OF THE ALMIGHTY

Meaning
The Holy Spirit is the life-giving breath
of God.

Application
The Holy Spirit is the source of life from God.
He is the one, through Christ, who connects
us to God. The words in both Hebrew and
Greek for "wind," "breath," and "spirit" all
have similar origins. The idea of flowing life-
giving air is what is meant.

Bible Reference
Job 33:4

COUNSELOR, COMFORTER

Meaning
The Holy Spirit comforts, counsels, and gives strength.

Application
Paraclete is the Greek word behind this name. It refers to an advocate, someone called alongside to strengthen and fight on behalf of another.

The Holy Spirit is our strength and comfort. We are to turn to him when we are in trouble and when we are weak, being assured that he intercedes with and for us.

Bible Reference
John 14:16, 26; 15:26; Romans 8:26

ETERNAL SPIRIT

Meaning
The Holy Spirit is eternal God.

Application
The Holy Spirit is the timeless Creator who loves us eternally. He is co-eternal with God the Father and God the Son.

Bible Reference
Hebrews 9:14

FREE SPIRIT

Meaning
The Holy Spirit is God's generous and willing spirit.

Application
Without God's Spirit who makes us willing to receive him, we would never be free from the prison of sin.

Bible Reference
Psalm 51:12

GOD

Meaning
The Holy Spirit is the Third Person of the Trinity. He is God.

Application
We are to understand that God is one in his essence, but three in Person.

Bible Reference
Acts 5:3–4

GOOD SPIRIT

Meaning
God's Good Spirit will teach and lead us in all that is good.

Application
We are not alone in the world. Christ's very own Spirit is with us to work all things for our good.

Bible Reference
Nehemiah 9:20; Psalm 143:10

HOLY SPIRIT

Meaning
God is Spirit and that Spirit is holy. He is the Spirit of holiness.

Application
The same Holy Spirit given to us for life is given to make us holy as well.

The term *Holy Ghost* is sometimes used in place of *Holy Spirit*. *Ghost* today has a negative idea attached to it. The use of the qualifier "holy" is to distinguish God's Spirit from evil spirits.

Bible Reference
Psalm 51:11; Luke 11:13; Ephesians 1:13; 4:30

LORD

Meaning
Like Jesus and the Father, the Holy Spirit is also addressed and worshiped as Lord.

Application
The lordship of the Spirit means we are to obey him and not grieve him.

Bible Reference
2 Corinthians 3:16–17

SPIRIT OF GOD

Meaning
The Holy Spirit is the Spirit of the Triune God.

Application
The Holy Spirit is the essence and core of the relationship between the Father and the Son.

Bible Reference
Genesis 1:2; 1 Corinthians 2:11; Job 33:4

POWER OF THE HIGHEST

Meaning
The Spirit is God's power, the greatest power there is.

Application
God's power, the Holy Spirit can accomplish things through us that we cannot do ourselves.

Bible Reference
Luke 1:35

SPIRIT OF MIGHT

Meaning
The Holy Spirit is the Spirit of Strength.

Application
Jesus told us he would give us the Power of the Spirit (Acts 1:8).

Bible Reference
Isaiah 11:2

Spirit of Counsel

Meaning
The Holy Spirit counsels and teaches us as we grow in Christ.

Application
Jesus is called the Wonderful Counselor (Isaiah 9:6). Just as the Holy Spirit led Jesus to the wilderness (Luke 4:1), he leads us to truth as our Counselor (John 14:26).

Bible Reference
Isaiah 11:2

Spirit of Glory

Meaning
The Spirit always gives glory to Christ.

Application
The Holy Spirit is shaping our lives into the glorious pattern of Christ.

Bible Reference
1 Peter 4:14

Spirit of Adoption

Meaning
He is the Spirit by which we are made God's children.

Application
We may actually refer to God as "Daddy" (*Abba* in Aramaic) or "Father" because we have Jesus' Spirit in us.

Bible Reference
Romans 8:15

Spirit of Burning

Meaning
The Spirit is God's fire of purification.

Application
God's Spirit cleanses and purifies from evil. The Spirit of God often appears as fire (Matthew 3:11; Acts 2:3).

Bible Reference
Isaiah 4:4

SPIRIT OF CHRIST (JESUS CHRIST)

Meaning
The Holy Spirit is Jesus' own spirit of love shared with the Father.

Application
The very same Spirit of love that the Father shares with the Son is now given to us (1 John 1:3).

Bible Reference
Romans 8:9; 1 Peter 1:11

SPIRIT OF TRUTH

Meaning
The Holy Spirit is about truth, not falsehood.

Application
Jesus said he is truth. We receive his Spirit of truth.

Bible Reference
John 14:17; 15:26

SPIRIT OF GRACE

Meaning
God's Spirit is a merciful spirit.

Application
Jesus accomplished the work of grace for us on the cross, but it is the Spirit who applies that grace to us by giving us faith.

Bible Reference
Zechariah 12:10; Hebrews 10:29

SPIRIT OF KNOWLEDGE

Meaning
The Spirit is the Spirit of clarity of mind.

Application
Jesus is the shoot from Jesse's stem—in other words, the Messiah—that Isaiah prophesied; Jesus had the fullness of the Spirit of knowledge.

Bible Reference
Isaiah 11:2

SPIRIT OF THE SON

Meaning
The Spirit is the Spirit of Jesus, the Son, whom he shares with the Father.

Application
The Spirit draws us into the love and fellowship that is between the Father and the Son.

Bible Reference
Galatians 4:6

SPIRIT OF WISDOM

Meaning
The Holy Spirit is wise.

Application
The Spirit is wise in the way he leads us. The Spirit is the source of all true wisdom.

Bible Reference
Isaiah 11:2; Ephesians 1:17

SPIRIT OF LIFE

Meaning
The Holy Spirit is life-giving (John 6:63).

Application
Jesus said he is life (John 14:6). His Spirit is the giver of that life.

Bible Reference
Romans 8:2

SPIRIT OF THE LIVING GOD

Meaning
The Holy Spirit is the Spirit of the God of life.

Application
God is called the Living God because he is life and the source of life through his Spirit to the world.

Bible Reference
2 Corinthians 3:3

SPIRIT OF PROPHECY

Meaning
It is the Holy Spirit who inspires true prophecy.

Application
The Spirit helps us understand God's Word.
All Scripture is inspired (God-breathed). The
Spirit is the breath of inspiration
(2 Timothy 3:16).

Bible Reference
Revelation 19:10

SPIRIT OF REVELATION

Meaning
God's spirit reveals his truth.

Application
Revelation comes from the Father through
Jesus by the Spirit who is the voice of God in
us.

Bible Reference
Ephesians 1:17

SPIRIT OF THE FATHER

Meaning
The Holy Spirit is the Spirit of the Father shared with Jesus.

Comments
The Spirit shared between the Father and Son, the Spirit of love, is now given to us.

Bible Reference
Matthew 10:20

SPIRIT OF THE FEAR OF THE LORD

Meaning
The Spirit is the Spirit of reverence toward the Lord.

Application
God is to be given awe and reverence. It is the Holy Spirit who inspires this attitude in us.

Bible Reference
Isaiah 11:2

SPIRIT OF THE LORD (GOD)

Meaning
The Spirit is the presence of the Lord.

Application
We are to worship and obey the Spirit as Lord.

Bible Reference
Acts 5:9

SPIRIT OF JUDGEMENT

Meaning
The Spirit of God brings conviction and judgement.

Application
God's Spirit discerns and divides good from evil. The Spirit convicts and judges the world (John 16:8).

Bible Reference
Isaiah 4:4; 28:6

SPIRIT OF UNDERSTANDING

Meaning
The Spirit is understanding itself.

Application
Jesus said the Spirit would help us understand (John 16:12–15).

Bible Reference
Isaiah 11:2

SPIRIT

Meaning
The Holy Spirit is sometimes simply called "Spirit."

Application
The Spirit is truly the source of all life; everything that exists does so only because of him.

Bible Reference
Matthew 4:1; John 3:6; 1 Timothy 4:1

SPIRIT OF YAHWEH, SPIRIT OF THE LORD YAHWEH

Meaning
The Spirit has the sacred name of God—Yahweh.

Application
The Spirit can be called by the sacred name because he is God. Jesus told his disciples to baptize in the name (singular) of the Father, Son, and Holy Spirit (Matthew 28:19).

Bible Reference
Isaiah 11:2; 61:1

TRINITY

WHAT CHRISTIANS BELIEVE ABOUT THE TRINITY

In the simplest of terms, Christians believe that there is only one God, and this one God exists as one essence in three Persons.

The three Persons are:
God the Father
God the Son (Jesus Christ)
God the Holy Spirit (also called the Holy Ghost)

The Persons are distinct:
The Father is not the Son.
The Son is not the Holy Spirit.
The Holy Spirit is not the Father.

God is one absolutely perfect divine Being in three Persons. His *being* is what God <u>is</u>, in relation to the universe he created. The three are called Persons because they relate to one another in personal ways.

Early Christians used this diagram to explain the Trinity. The Father, Son, and Holy Spirit are all God, but they are not three names for the same Person.

When Christians talk about believing in one God in three Persons (the Trinity), they do NOT mean:
1 God in 3 Gods, or
3 Persons in 1 Person, or
3 Persons in 3 Gods, or
1 Person in 3 Gods

Rather, they mean:
  1 God in 3 Persons

Therefore,

The Father is God—the first Person of the Trinity.

The Son is God—the second Person of the Trinity.

The Holy Spirit is God—the third Person of the Trinity. (The title "Holy Ghost" is an older English expression for "Holy Spirit." Each is an acceptable translation of the phrase in the Bible.)

WHY DO CHRISTIANS BELIEVE IN THE TRINITY?

The Bible clearly teaches that there is only one God, yet all three Persons are called God.

There is only one God
• *Hear, O Israel: The LORD our God is one LORD.* (Deuteronomy 6:4)

- *Before me there was no God formed, neither shall there be after me. (Isaiah 43:10; 44:6–8; 45:5)*

The Father is God

- *Grace be unto you, and peace, from God our Father, and from the Lord Jesus Christ. (1 Corinthians 1:3; 8:6; Ephesians 4:4–6)*

The Son is God

- *The Word was God. (John 1:1–5, 14)* Jesus is identified as "the Word."

- *I and the Father are one. (John 10:30–33)*

- Jesus' disciple Thomas addressed Jesus as "My Lord and my God," (John 20:28)

  Jesus did not tell Thomas he was mistaken; instead Jesus accepted these titles. Other people in Scripture, notably Paul and Barnabas, refused to accept worship as gods (Acts 14).

You Might Also Like

NAMES OF GOD
& OTHER BIBLE STUDIES

Names of God & Other Bible Studies is one of the best-selling Bible studies on the Names of God available today. Includes optional fill-in-the-blank Bible study guide. Perfect for small groups, Sunday school classes, church groups, and for personal study.

Names of God & Other Bible Studies gives you enough basic Bible teaching to use in a six-week Bible study or small group or class.

ISBN: 9781596362031